THE VICTORIAN DENTIST

Gill Munton

Contents

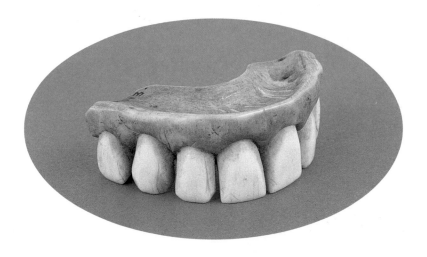

OXFORD
UNIVERSITY PRESS

The dentist's chair

This is a very old chair.

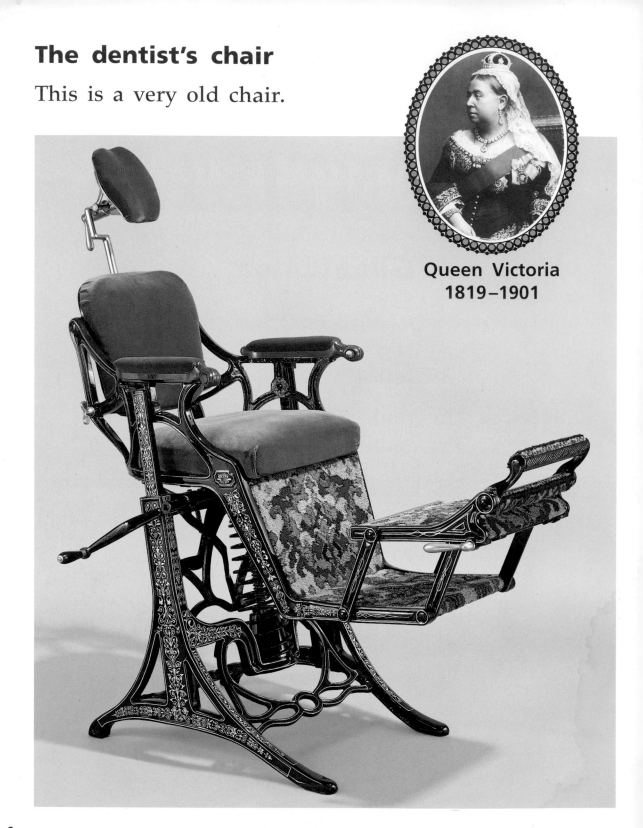

Queen Victoria
1819–1901

A dentist used it in Victorian times.

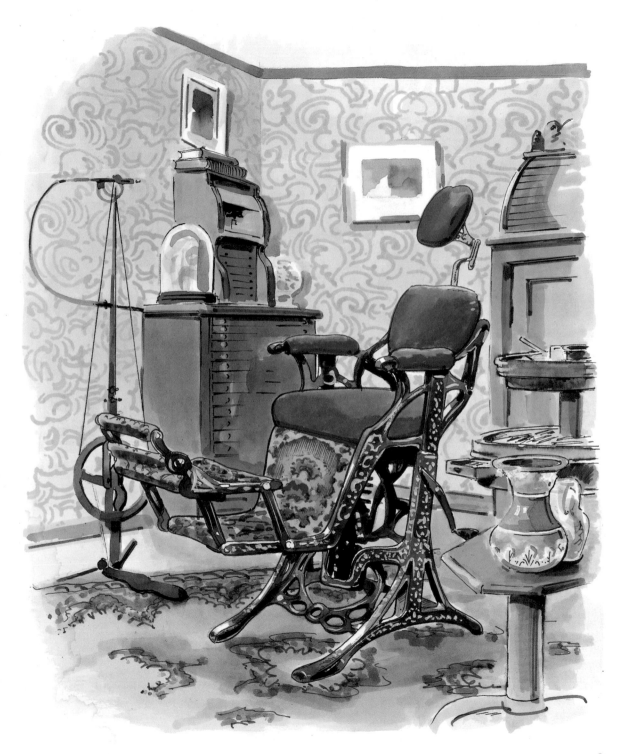

The dentist's tools

This is his box of tools.

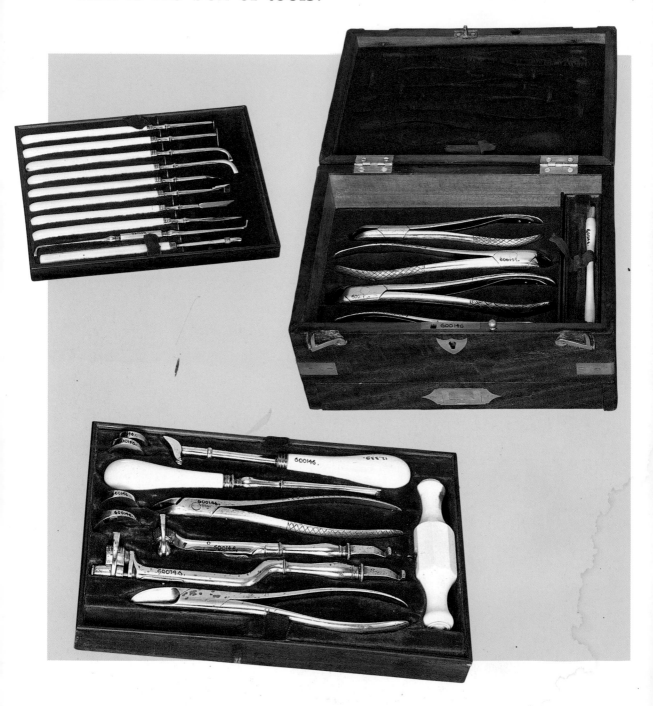

The tools are made of bone and metal.

These are his mirrors.

mouth mirror

hand mirror

He looked at people's back teeth
with the mouth mirror.

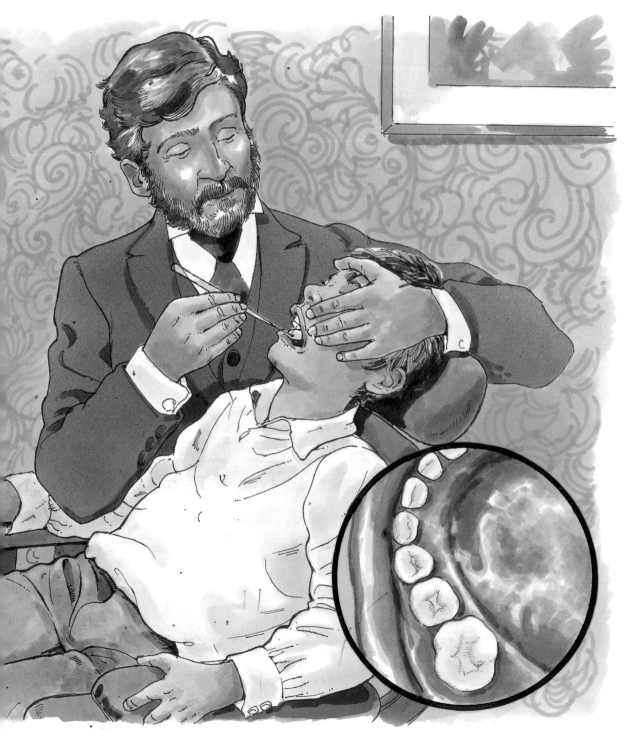

This is his drill.

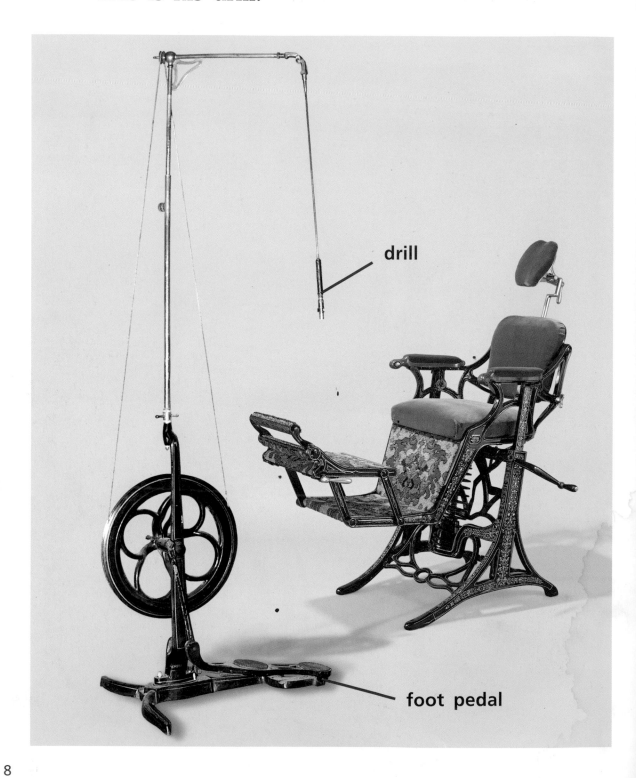

drill

foot pedal

He made it work with his foot.

This is his gold.

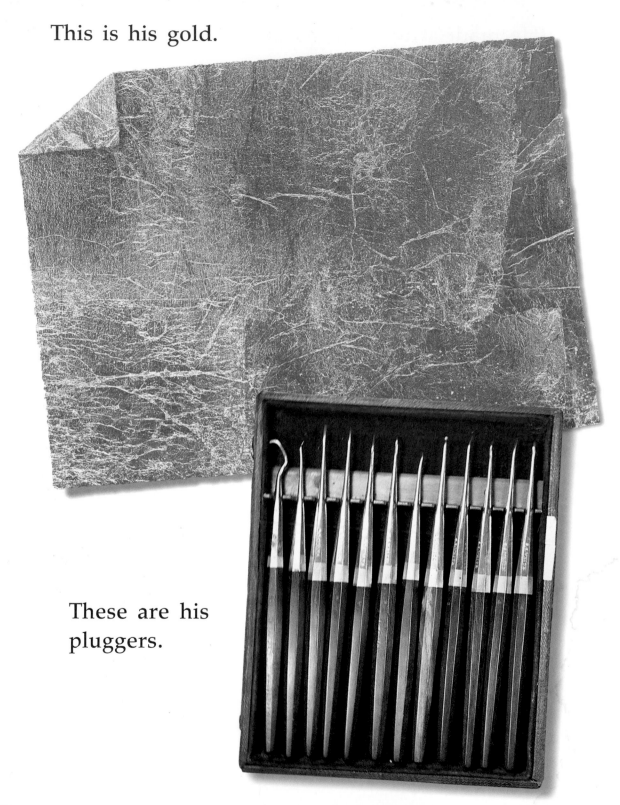

These are his
pluggers.

He made fillings with these.

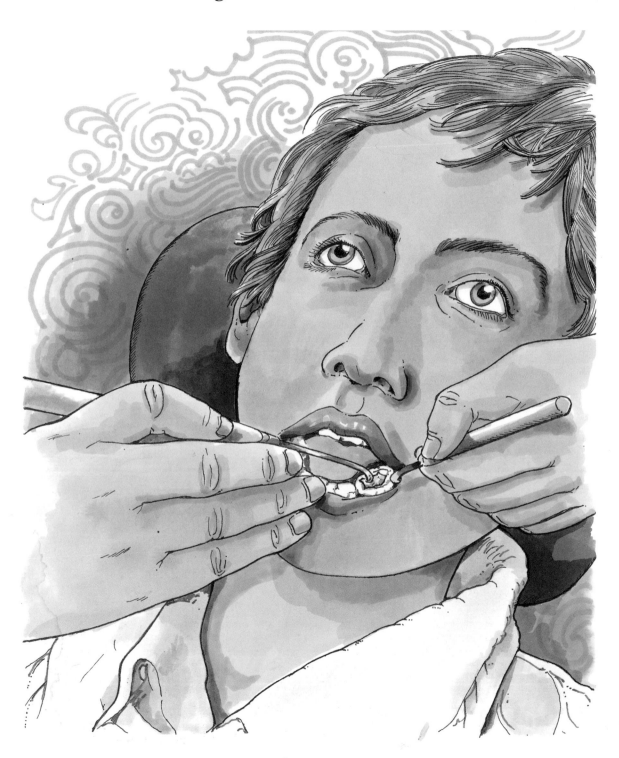

He pulled out teeth with this.

These are Victorian
false teeth.

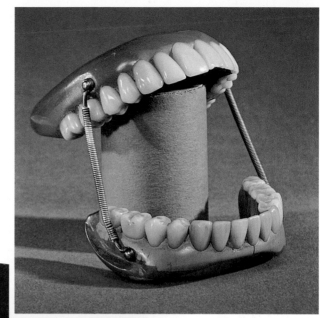

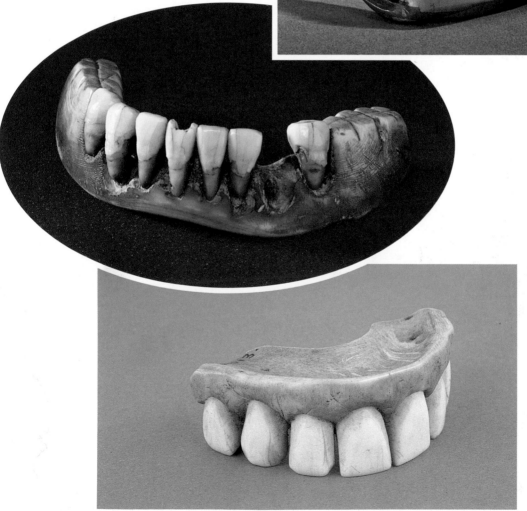

Looking after teeth

The dentist told people to look after their teeth.

He told them to use this . . .

. . . and this.